Weirdo and Willy

By Marcy Pusey

Illustrated by Ferdinando C. Rihi

Philip —
Weird is cool!
Be as "weird" as God
made you to be — it's lovely!

Cover design and illustrations by Ferdinando Christian Rihi

Hardback ISBN-13:978-1-948283-09-0
Paperback ISBN-13: 978-1-948283-10-6
eBook ISBN-13:978-1-948283-11-3

Library of Congress Control Number: 2019939381

Pusey, Marcy

Weirdo and Willy / Marcy Pusey
Willy is taunted by his classmates for being weird, until one day, a "weirdo" actually shows up! The creature wants to play! Thus begins a tale of unlikely friendship: Weirdo and Willy find the companionship they've been missing in the most unlikely of people... er, creatures.

ISBN-(hc) 13: 978-1-948283-09-0

DEDICATION

To every child who's been called a hurtful name, this is your name:

Loved

You are worthy of all the affection of Heaven.

—M.P.

But on Thursday...

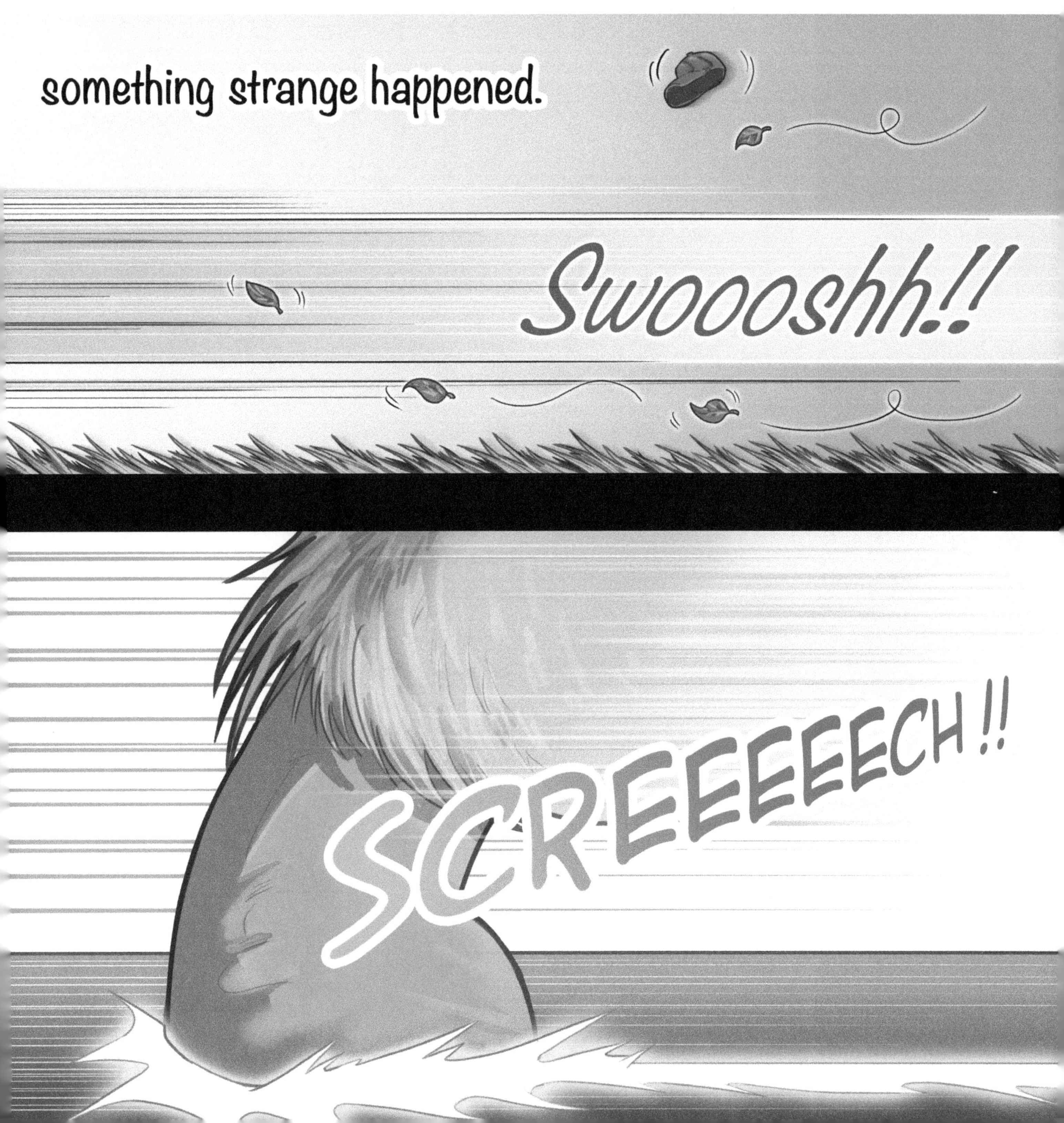
something strange happened.
Swoooshh!!
SCREEEEECH!!

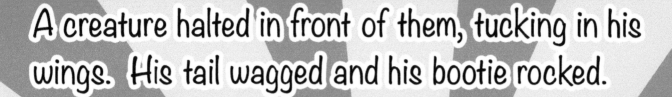

A creature halted in front of them, tucking in his wings. His tail wagged and his bootie rocked.

The kids' teeth chattered and knees wobbled. Willy stammered,

But before Willy could finish,
Weirdo swung Willy onto his back and said,

The name-callers ran in every direction, tripping and shoving, shouting and fleeing.

Weirdo flew so fast that Willy's cheeks wiggled in the wind. Weirdo tapped one of the fleeing kids on the shoulder.

Swoooooooshhh...!!!

You're *it!*

Ahhh!

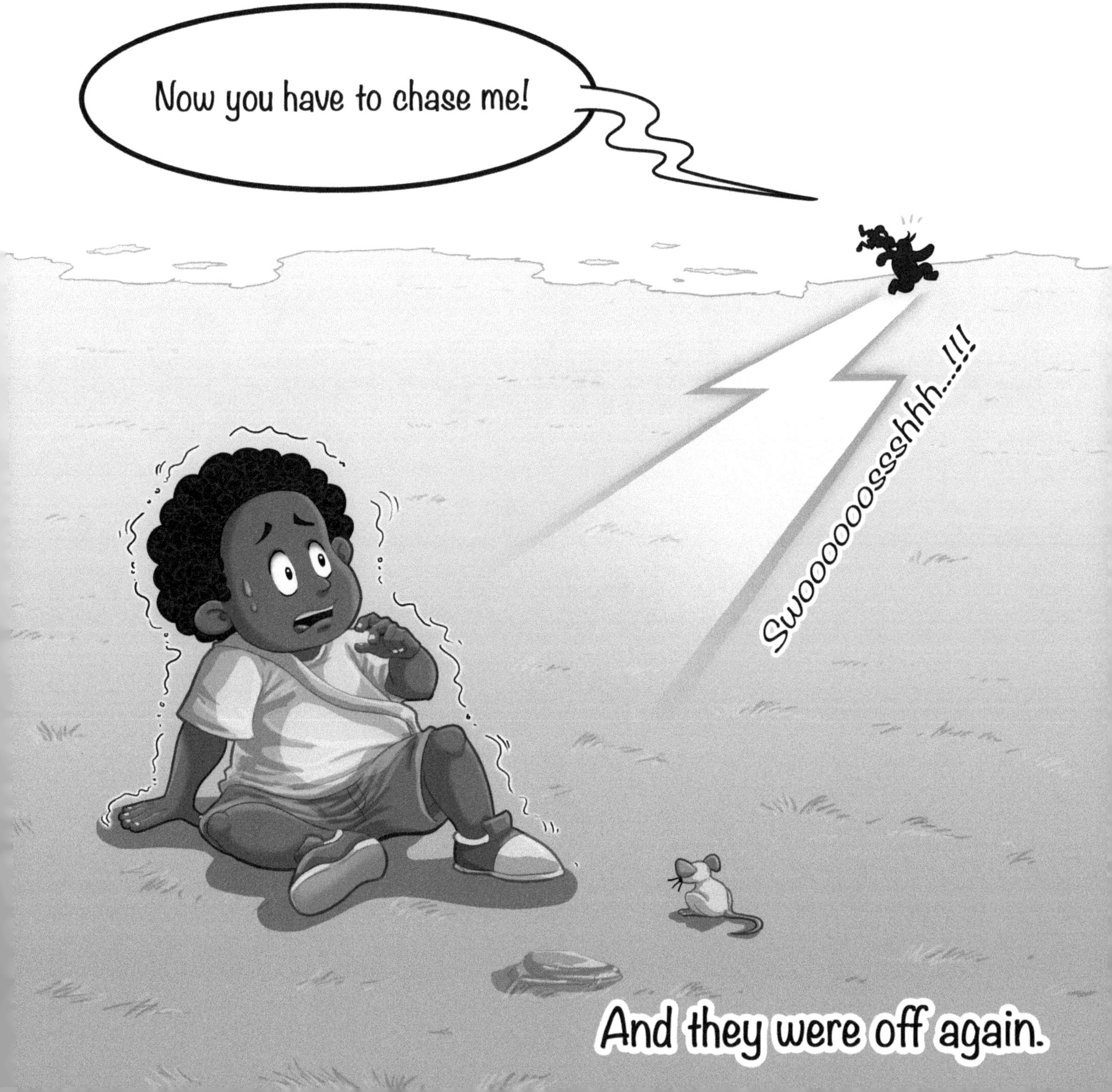

And they were off again.

Weirdo swept through the town,

giggling as he escaped from...

No one.

Willy slid off of Weirdo's back. Sobs turned into sniffles.

Weirdo blew his nose into his armpit.

Willy couldn't decide if Weirdo was terrible or terrific.

Well,
you *are* a little strange.

I mean, you have drool...

everywhere.

And your teeth are...

big.

Weirdo howled through tears.

Weirdo took a good look at Willy. His tummy growled.

Willy put his arm around Weirdo.

I have an idea.

Willy and Weirdo sat at their nicely prepared picnic bench and waited.

The wind blew. Crickets chirped.

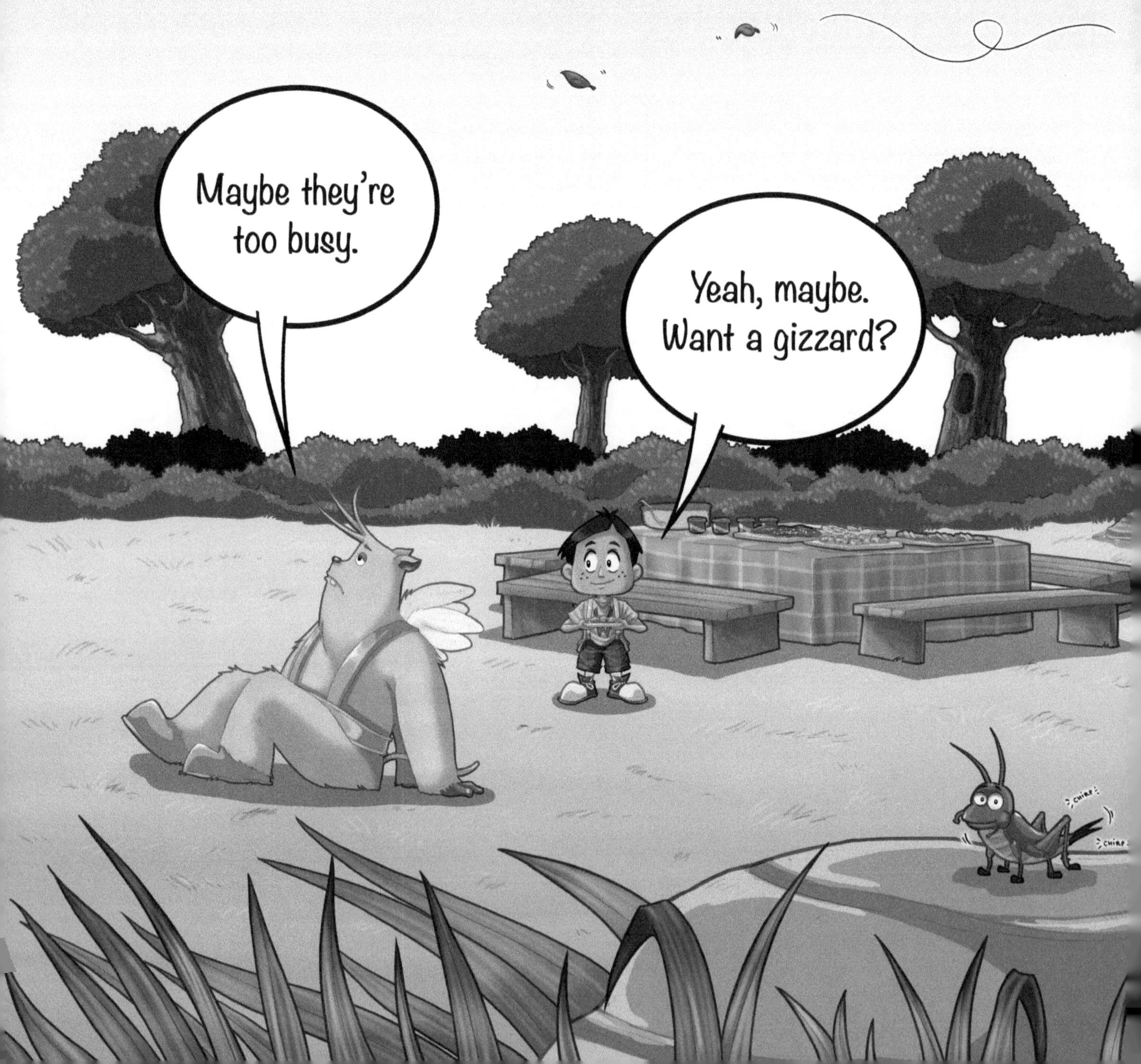

Weirdo took a big bite.

Willy poured Weirdo some pickle-punch.

Suddenly, a head poked up at the end of the table. A hand reached across the table and grabbed a caramel-dipped frog tongue.

Another kid joined the party.

And another.

Then another.

But this time they tried the food, the drinks, and the laughter.

Willy looked around.

Willy jumped up and cleaned his face in Weirdo's armpit. "Got it!" he declared.

But Weirdo couldn't hear him over his own laughter.

Meanwhile, in a town not too far away,
Claudia is a Clod-hopper!
Claudia is a Clod-hopper!
Claudia is a Clod-hopper!
the ground began to rattle.

ABOUT THE AUTHOR

Marcy M. Pusey loves her family, exploring the world, reading, Cherry-Pepsi Slurpees, the ocean, Wonder Woman, and looking for castles to visit. She also loves writing stories that encourage and build up others. Marcy is a Certified Rehabilitation Counselor and the best-selling author of books for children and adults. Marcy is originally from California but now lives in the Black Forest of Germany with her husband and younger children.

Follow Marcy's work at www.marcypusey.com.

More books from Marcy Pusey

Available wherever books are sold
or may be directly ordered from
www.marcypusey.com.

CPSIA information can be obtained
at www.ICGtesting.com
Printed in the USA
BVHW020448120619
550778BV00004B/22/P

Diwali and Dipawali
Hindu festival of light, celebrated for several days each year in India. The most important day of the celebration is Lakshmi Puja, which falls on Amavasya.

It is a day dedicated to **Lakshmi** (goddess of happiness and prosperity) or **Lakshmi** and **Ganesi**. Dipawali literally means "**row of lamps**" (from the words dipa = "lamp" and awali = "row").

The word **Dipawali** refers to the olive lamps made of fired clay that are lit in front of each house to welcome **Lakshmi**. The lamps symbolize the victory of **light over darkness**, good over evil.

The setting of the festival is enhanced by **fireworks** and **floral decorations**.

Diwali is celebrated on a grand scale, accompanied by numerous cultural events.It is one of the **most important** traditional holidays celebrated in India.

It is an opportunity to meet with family and friends who are given sweets.

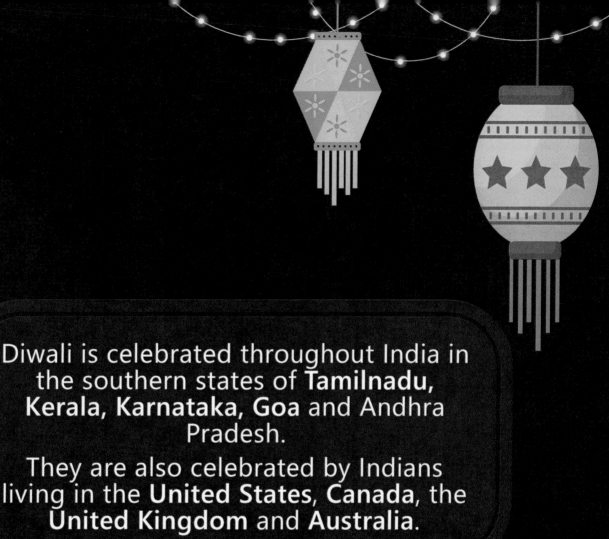

Diwali is celebrated throughout India in the southern states of **Tamilnadu, Kerala, Karnataka, Goa** and Andhra Pradesh.

They are also celebrated by Indians living in the **United States, Canada**, the **United Kingdom** and **Australia**.

According to the **Hindu calendar** (in which the lunar month begins after the full moon), the amavasya marking Diwali will be the **15th day** of the month of **kartika**.

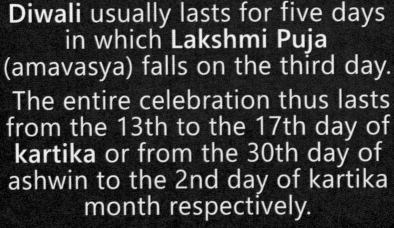

Diwali usually lasts for five days in which **Lakshmi Puja** (amavasya) falls on the third day.

The entire celebration thus lasts from the 13th to the 17th day of **kartika** or from the 30th day of ashwin to the 2nd day of kartika month respectively.

In the state of **Maharashtra**, Diwali celebrations last longer.

Starting a day earlier, while in **Gujarat** it starts two days earlier and ends three days later.

Items used during this wonderful ceremony

Diya literally a lamp. In Hindi also referred to as **diya**, **dip**, **dipak**, **diwa**. Although etymologically all the terms mean the same thing, the modern distinction is usually between disposable clay lamps, and brass lamps used permanently in the home or temple.
Both types are usually small oil lamps, made famous by the great "Festival of Light" called Diwali or Dipawali.

DIYA (LAMP)

CANDLES & FIREWORKS

Diwali Candles & Fireworks

is interpreted as a way to ward off all **evil spirits** as well as add to the festive mood. In addition, this ritual may also be linked to the tradition of paying respect to ancestors. The Diwali night's lights and fireworks represent a celebratory and symbolic farewell to the departed **ancestral souls**.

Aloo Bonda, Potato Bonda, Bonda.

Popular snack which is also known as mumbai batata vada or bombay potato vada recipe is a deep fried spicy potato dumpling. It is prepared with spiced mashed potato baji which is then coated with besan batter and then deep fried till golden crisp.

ALOO BONDA

KANDEEL

Kandeel
are traditional lanterns, hung for up to a month from the beginning of **Diwali**. **Kandeel** come in a variety of shapes and sizes, **including stars**, **lanterns**, **cubes** and **globes**. Often referred to as Diwali lanterns, they have evolved over the years and are now commonly used with electric lights.

Rangoli

(from Sanskrit: ranga + avalli "band of colors") - a decoration made of colorful, small elements, usually created in front of the entrance to houses. The use of perishable materials (usually sand, grains or flowers) is a symbol of the impermanence of the world, referred to by the word maya. Rangoli are also an important part of Hindu festivals, especially Diwali.

RANGOLI

Happy

Diwali

Made in the USA
Las Vegas, NV
15 September 2023

77588650R00019